Inspiring women

ARUNIMA SINHA

THE MOUNTAINEER

Written by

Kunal Kapsime

Illustrated by

Ruby Lam

This is the story of a courageous woman called Arunima, who overcame many challenges to achieve her goal.

Arunima was born in 1989 in a small town in India.
She had an elder sister and a younger brother.
She lost her father when she was three years old.

Arunima loved to play sports as a child. She played soccer in her school team and even played volleyball for her college at the national level.

But, in those days there were limited opportunities for women in sports in India. So, she had to stop pursuing sports to focus on getting a job.

At the age of 24, she was traveling in a train when some bad guys tried to rob her. She tried to stop them, but she was thrown off the train. Due to this accident, she lost her left leg. She was given a prosthetic leg which could help her walk.

While Arunima was healing, she read about Mount
Everest, the highest mountain peak in the world.
She also learned that no one with a prosthetic leg
had ever climbed Mount Everest.

Arunmia set her goal to climb Mount Everest.
She wanted to prove that she could reach the top of
the world, especially to those people who thought a
woman and an amputee couldn't do it.

When she discussed the plan with the doctors, they discouraged her. They told her that climbing a mountain was not going to be easy with her prosthetic leg.

MT.EVEREST

But, Arunima had a strong will and was determined to do it. She met with Bechendri Pal, who was the first woman from India to climb Mount Everest.

Pal listened to Arunima's plan. She told her that by making this difficult decision, Arunima has already conquered Mount Everest in her heart.

Her encouraging words lit a spark inside Arunima.
She decided to give it a go and started her training.
She trained non-stop for 18 months and climbed several
smaller mountains to improve her skills.

Just two years after her surgery, Arunima decided to try to climb the highest peak in the world, Mount Everest.

Climbing high mountains requires a long hike to a base camp. She faced a lot of pain and difficulty on her way to the base camp. Seeing her struggling, her team advised her to return. But, Arunima did not give up.

 She decided to continue and successfully reached the peak of Mount Everest after 52 days. Arunima was very happy to have achieved her goal!

Arunima was not yet completely out of danger. On her way back, she ran out of oxygen and fell to the ground. As she lay gasping for breath, her Sherpa found an extra tank of oxygen that another climber had left behind.

Arunima was able to use that oxygen and was able to return to the base camp safely. Later on she said "It is my firmest conviction that luck will favor those who have the drive and the tenacity to win."

Arunima did not stop there, and made it her dream to climb the highest peak in each of the seven continents. She is the world's first female amputee to do so.

Elbrus
Russia- Europe
Everest
Nepal and China- Asia
Kilimanjaro
Tanzania- Africa
Kosciuszko
Australia

In 2015, she was awarded Padma Shri, the fourth highest civilian award in India. She is also the recipient of the highest mountaineering award in India.

She currently runs a charitable organization to help educate and develop skills among specially-abled people, to help them achieve their goals and become self-dependent. Arunima's story is of tenacity and strong will and demonstrates that anyone can achieve their goal if they set their mind to it.